CREATIVE POWER:
30 DAYS OF CREATIVE AFFIRMATIONS

BY MIKE BRENNAN

All rights reserved. No part of this book may be reproduced in any form without permission from the author and publisher.

Copyright © 2024 by Mike Brennan

Design by Mike Brennan

Published by DCH Resources

ISBN 9798873873807

When I was a kid in the 80's, I was a fan of He-Man and the Masters of the Universe. I couldn't watch enough of the cartoon show, and had all the action figures. (Yes, even Cringer AKA Battle Cat.)

As artists, writers, musicians, and creators, so much of our time is spent navigating the intricate landscapes of our minds. It's a place of wonder, a playground for ideas, and sometimes, a battlefield where self-doubt and mental health battles can wage. In the whirlwind of our creative journeys, there's a tool that often gets overlooked but can be a game-changer: *daily affirmations*.

Ever notice how He-Man didn't just raise his fists when facing his enemy, Skeletor? Nope, he held aloft the Power Sword, declared "***I HAVE THE POWER!***", and BAM! Instant muscle-bound hero ready to kick butt. Well, guess what? You have your own Power Sword, my friend, and it's called affirmations.

Our minds are both our greatest ally and fiercest critic. As creatives, we invest a substantial amount of our time and energy in the realms of imagination and introspection. It's a beautiful space, but it can also be a challenging one. The constant dance between inspiration and doubt can take a toll on our mental health.

Enter daily affirmations – those little positivity phrases that act as gentle reminders of our worth and potential. Affirmations are like the warm hug we all need on a tough day. They serve as beacons of encouragement, steering us away from the treacherous waters of self-doubt and guiding us towards the shores of a growth mindset.

Why Daily Affirmations?

1. Positive Thinking: Affirmations help cultivate a positive mindset. They gently redirect our thoughts, turning the spotlight away from self-criticism and towards the possibilities that lie ahead.

2. Growth Mindset: Creative endeavors are a journey, not a destination. Affirmations foster a growth mindset, encouraging us to see challenges as opportunities for learning and growth.

3. Mental Health Guardians: In the solitary world of creativity, mental health battles can be a formidable adversary. Affirmations become our armor, shielding us from the impact of negativity and offering a refuge of positivity.

Now, I know there might be a skeptic in the room, rolling their eyes at the mention of affirmations. To be honest, that was me for the longest time. (I am from New York, after all…)

"Isn't that just wishful thinking?" they might say. Well, to the skeptics, I say this: **affirmations are not about wishful thinking; they are about intentional thinking.** They are the conscious choice to direct our thoughts towards the positive, the empowering, and the uplifting.

Consider this – if we can spend hours perfecting our craft, why not invest a few minutes each day in perfecting our mindset? Affirmations are like daily exercises for our mental muscles, strengthening our resilience and fostering a sense of self-belief.

Creativity is a journey, and affirmations are the compass that helps us navigate its twists and turns. So, let's make a commitment to our creative selves – a commitment to spend a few moments each day immersed in the warmth of affirmations, affirming our worth, and setting the tone for a day filled with positivity and growth.

Remember, the world needs your unique voice, your vibrant stories, your innovative solutions. So grab your Power Sword of affirmations, and unleash your inner He-Man. The universe awaits your creative mastery!

"The world is full of magic things, patiently waiting for our senses to grow sharper."

- W.B. Yeats

MY IMAGINATION KNOWS NO BOUNDS, AND I AM CONSTANTLY INSPIRED.

"Like fingerprints on clay, each artist leaves their indelible mark, their unique story."

- Henry Ward Beecher

I EMBRACE THE UNIQUE PERSPECTIVE I BRING TO THE WORLD.

"The only time I feel alive is when I'm painting."

- Vincent van Gogh

I TRUST THE PROCESS OF MY CREATIVE JOURNEY.

"I am seeking. I am striving. I am in it with all my heart."

- *Vincent van Gogh*

MY MISTAKES LEAD TO GROWTH, AND I CELEBRATE THEM IN MY PROCESS.

"Art enables us to find ourselves and lose ourselves at the same time."

- Thomas Merton

I AM OPEN TO NEW POSSIBILITIES AND PERSPECTIVES.

"Don't think about making art, just get it done. Let everyone else decide if it's good or bad, whether they love it or hate it. While they are deciding, make even more art."

- Andy Warhol

MY CREATIVITY FLOWS EFFORTLESSLY, GUIDED BY MY ARTISTIC INSTINCTS.

---

*"Art should comfort
the disturbed and disturb
the comfortable."*

- Cesar A. Cruz

I AM A VESSEL OF INSPIRATION, AND MY WORK RESONATES WITH OTHERS.

"Creativity takes courage."

- Henri Matisse

I TRUST MY INTUITION TO GUIDE ME IN CREATING MEANINGFUL ART.

"To be an artist is to believe in life."

- Henry Moore

I RELEASE SELF-DOUBT AND EMBRACE THE CONFIDENCE WITHIN ME.

"Where focus goes, energy flows."

- Tony Robbins

I ATTRACT POSITIVE ENERGY THAT FUELS MY CREATIVE SPIRIT.

"There are a thousand ways to be beautiful. Be brave. Be you."

- Erin Hanson

MY CREATIVITY IS A GIFT, AND I SHARE IT WITH THE WORLD AUTHENTICALLY.

"Every artist was first an amateur."

- Ralph Waldo Emerson

I AM OPEN TO RECEIVING INSPIRATION FROM UNEXPECTED SOURCES.

"Painting is just another way of keeping a diary."

- Pablo Picasso

I TRUST THAT MY CREATIVE ENDEAVORS WILL MAKE A POSITIVE IMPACT.

"Art is not what you see, but what you make others see."

- Edgar Degas

I AM IN CONTROL OF MY CREATIVE PROCESS, AND I TRUST THE TIMING OF MY SUCCESS.

"The best artist has no conception that a marble block does not contain within itself."

- Michelangelo

I LET GO OF COMPARISON AND CELEBRATE MY UNIQUE ARTISTIC VOICE.

"This dance between me and art, a tango of surrender and sacrifice, a whispered promise I keep with every breath."

- Vincent van Gogh

MY CREATIVITY IS A REFLECTION OF MY INNER JOY AND PASSION.

> *"Creativity is contagious, pass it on."*
>
> *- Albert Einstein*

I AM CONSTANTLY EVOLVING AND GROWING AS A CREATIVE INDIVIDUAL.

"Art is born out of struggles. Every great artist is first of all a great wrestler."

- Honoré de Balzac

I TRUST THAT CHALLENGES ARE OPPORTUNITIES FOR CREATIVE BREAKTHROUGHS.

> *"The artist's vision,
> a prism refracting the
> world through the lens
> of their soul."*
>
> *- Henry Ward Beecher*

MY CREATIVITY IS A POWERFUL FORCE THAT TRANSFORMS MY REALITY.

"Every single flower you see is a miracle, and that also applies to you and me."

- Walt Whitman

I AM GRATEFUL FOR THE INSPIRATION THAT SURROUNDS ME EVERY DAY.

"Art enables us to find ourselves and lose ourselves at the same time."

- Thomas Merton

I AM A MAGNET FOR CREATIVE IDEAS AND INNOVATIVE SOLUTIONS.

> *"To be an artist is to believe in life."*
>
> *- Henry Moore*

I AM A MAGNET FOR CREATIVE IDEAS AND INNOVATIVE SOLUTIONS.

"With every brushstroke, I chase a horizon that recedes, forever yearning for the next masterpiece."

- Vincent van Gogh

I TRUST THE LIMITLESS POSSIBILITIES OF MY CREATIVE IMAGINATION.

"Let us become the words whispered into the wind, carried on wings of song to ignite a constellation of hearts."

- Victoria Erickson

MY CREATIVITY IS A SOURCE OF INSPIRATION FOR OTHERS.
―――――――――――――

"Art is not freedom from discipline, but disciplined freedom."

- John F. Kennedy

I AM CONFIDENT IN EXPRESSING MY UNIQUE CREATIVE VISION.
───────────────────

"Difficulty is what wakes up the genius."

- Nassim Nicholas Taleb

I AM RESILIENT IN THE FACE OF CREATIVE CHALLENGES.

"Art is alchemy, transforming the artist's inner fire into tangible beauty for the world to see."

- Henry Ward Beecher

I TRUST THE WISDOM OF MY CREATIVE INSTINCTS.

"There is no end to creativity."

- John F. Kennedy

MY CREATIVITY KNOWS NO LIMITS, AND I AM CONSTANTLY EVOLVING.

"Variety is the spice of life."

- William Shakespeare

I AM OPEN TO EXPLORING NEW MEDIUMS AND TECHNIQUES.

> *"Art is the only way to run away without leaving home."*
>
> *- Twyla Tharp*

I TRUST THAT MY CREATIVE WORK HAS A POSITIVE IMPACT ON THE WORLD.

WRITE YOUR OWN AFFIRMATIONS:

WRITE YOUR OWN AFFIRMATIONS:

ABOUT THE AUTHOR

Mike Brennan is a Creative Consultant and Communicator telling stories on pages and stages integrating creativity, innovation, and productivity. Mike has worked with clients such as Heineken, and Chase Bank, and has had his art featured in the Ronald McDonald House and the I.D.E.A. Museum in Mesa, Arizona.

Mike helps fellow creatives, organizations, and entrepreneurs leverage simple, practical steps for putting more innovation into their lives and businesses through his signature Daily Creative Process. He shares key methods and principles from his over ten-year daily creative practice and utilizes that experience to help businesses use creativity through time management, goal-driven creativity, and a sustainable way to make innovating a part of their daily life and work.

For more visit: *www.MikeBrennan.me*

OTHER TITLES AVAILABLE

Make Fun A Habit: The Creative PLAYbook For Making Life And Work Fun Again
www.MakeFunAHabit.com

Daily Creative Habit Journal
www.DailyCreativeHabit.com

Sign up for the Daily Creative Habit newsletter:
www.DailyCreativeHabit.com

Made in the USA
Middletown, DE
25 January 2024